dreams
W IN W
soy sauce

Ro.

TIA CHUCHA PRESS, CHICAGO

Grateful acknowledgements are made to *The Yale Observer*, *Streams*, and *Power*, where some of these poems appeared. Further acknowledgements to Michael Warr and the Guild Complex, William King and Spices, Leigh Jones and Club Lower Links, Cabaret Voltaire, Café Classico and to the Kenté Circle of Diaspora for airing many of these pieces.

Printed in the United States of America

Cover Art: *Dreams* © 1991 by Muhammad Ahmad

Cover Photo: Joshua B. Dreyfus

Design: Jane Kremsreiter

Typography: Susan Dühl

First Printing

ISBN: 0-9624287-7-9

Library of Congress Catalogue Card Number: 91-67066

Published by:
Tia Chucha Press
PO Box 476969
Chicago, IL 60647-6969

Distributed by:
Independent Literary Publishers Association
PO Box 816
Oak Park, IL 60303
(800) 242-4572

This project is partially supported by a grant from the City of Chicago— Department of Cultural Affairs, a state agency, the Illinois Arts Council and the National Endowment for the Arts.

This book is dedicated in loving memory to
Michael G. Cooke
friend, mentor, scholar, anchoring voice

∎

To Mum, for her guidance and praeternatural strength.

To Daddy and Mummy, for their love, pride and courage.

To Andrea, Lee, Karen and Kim—keep on moving.

Hail, back a Yard, the Folkeses:
Gloria Mercedes, James Sylvestre, Alwyn, Hubert, Sherrelle,
Terrell, Aunt Pal, O'neil, Roy, Carl Daniel, Peter, Totlyn, Juanita,
Jascinta, John, Michelle, Andrew;
the Joneses: Noel, Rose, William, Franklyn
plus the Holmes, Grandison, Anderson, Campbell, Bennett,
Scaaffee, White, Wilmot, and Witter families.

Hail others in Preston, Port Maria, Nannytown, Oracabesa,
St. Andrews, Kingston, Mandeville, Ochie and Mo'bay.

A note of thanks to inspiring friends:
Angela Shannon, Alison Lynn, Beatrice Sibblies,
Blake Koh, Bruce Van Spiva, Byron Auguste,
Chris Kutz, Chris Pitter, Deborah Sutter, Don Chen,
Greg Thomson, Heather Roberts, Carlton Henry Reid,
Hiro Aragaki, Howard Cohen, Jason Rubinstein,
Jean Jung, Jenna Deveza Michaels, Joel Obermayer,
Judith Oriol, Kel Lee Tice, Kenneth Norris, Lily Tsong,
Lina Han, Manuel Cenita Jimenez, Maxim Thorne,
Mitty Owens, Petria May, Seth MacLowry,
Shannon Carey, Sheila Deitz.

And mentors: Marie Borroff, Carmine Giordano,
Brian Hieggelke, John Hollander, bell hooks,
Gladys and Robert Levy, Michael Manley, Luis Rodriguez,
Ngugi wa Thing'o, Derek Walcott, Michael Warr,
and others too who have nurtured me.

Special thanks to Joseph Clark and his Art Werk Gallery,
Raul Niño, Marvin Tate, Maeola Mack, and Trinity.
I could not be living without all of you.

Guidance.

1

BLACK, ANTI-BLACK

2

CALLING OUT

3

MARROW TO MOUTH

BLACK
ANTI-BLACK

When I was a child in Jamaica, my schoolmates would come to our house on Saturdays to watch television. The same staple that sustained North American audiences was also offered to us. In the morning there were the cartoons whose elastic heroes assumed any elemental shape or essence. We drew strength from these figures, emulating them with utmost abandon. For example, all would take turns on my tricycle, going to the top of a hill and blazing down at uncontrollable speeds to crash in leaf heaps.

Whereas the cartoons were just silhouettes, the afternoon shows showed us the incarnate invincibility of the makers' heroes. We learned the culture and views of the tourists, distilled in the flicks they made and how they made them. All martial arts were kung fu and karate, one and the same, and they dominated early Saturday afternoons. With their water-slaps and guttural jerks, Bruce Lee and Chuck Norris showed us the vocabulary of the Chinese (all Asians were Chinese)—all that mysticism and smoke, and those secret glances.

In the early evening the one station available to the island featured westerns. My schoolmates and I had become so familiar with the scripts that we knew all the lines and scenes which were to unfold—even though we would not miss any episodes. My grandmother's curried goat, rice, peas, pineapples, breadfruit, carrot juice and rum cake would awaken armies in my stomach but I always watched the tube till the very end: when the battle is nearly won and there is a breathtaking setback (we would all put our hands over our mouths and gasp), the Apache would loom with his huge axe like a vulture over Ms. Daisy (all Native Americans were Alfalfa-like Apaches sprouting feathers from their brains; their only word, aside from incessant martial cackling, was the oath "How!"—as children we wondered why they would take an oath whenever they met each other). The leading man would then use his last bullet/only leg/injured arm/ etc. to rescue Ms. Daisy with ultimate and vengeful efficiency—a quick blow and the cymbals settled. The grateful heroine, bent over like a flower to sunlight, would glow in the camera before they "milked," or as I later learned in Brooklyn, "tongued down."

In fact, I later learned so many things in Brooklyn—courage, kindness and wintry isolation—that I cannot delineate my selves. One week after we landed at Kennedy (I could now watch all the westerns I wanted), on one of the rare occasions that my parents allowed their teenage son to leave the house (to fetch groceries), I saw a "senior citizen" get mugged. Her assailant bore down hard, not simply snatching her purse, but striking this octogenarian in the face repeatedly. I was ice-still—struck-dumb. All the elder people I had known in my life commanded tremendous respect—they were the mothers and fathers of the culture. In fact Mum, the greatest of all great grandmothers, could have been that woman—aside from her thin skin. The New York tabloids could have had a field day if they were at the scene ("Dominican Youth Brutally Bangs Park Slope Grandma") but there was no media-intense focus or exorcism. The memory is all private, all blistering.

I quickly learned other things too about my new country—the real history behind those happy-step westerns and martial arts movements; and I was surprised to find Black people here and even more surprised at the way Black people of all stripes regarded or discarded each other. I began to see the dept of how my experience was a reaction to these things. Even though my life was determined from beyond anonymous club walls—directed from beyond as if my life were some movie—I always knew the greatness of our heritage. With my maturation Stateside, I tried to move more and more behind the camera, behind the eight-ball or whatever else signifies that kind of vision or self-realization. I recognized the extent to which my entire world-view was colored (or bleached) by tourists—from how grandly I thought about the Thames, Queen Victoria, Henry Morgan and Lord Cromwell to how country and classical music had become the only musical genres I listened to, to the very way my parents regarded reggae and the Jamaican vernacular. My pride in a strong heritage of struggle and resistance was challenged on all fronts—my history now myth, lore, wishful thinking, if acknowledged at all.

Whereas all Jamaicans are culturally black, even the most stoosh households in the hills of St. Andrews, and whereas after the television, movies, and classroom lectures, we return to a warm, affirmative milieu, the reality in this country was decidedly what Public Enemy calls "An Anti-Nigger Machine." So overwhelming was this sentiment that I was a "man" at thirteen, when we landed at Kennedy. Based on the way people treated me on the streets, I was thus responsible for criminal activities I did not know about.

In my continuing growth, I was able to overcome the ignorance which divides African-Americans from Africans born elsewhere. Such growth occurs only after we come to know the glorious history and gallantry of this culture—not the hatred exported by American images. We must know how it has determined the culture of these United States, not just in the arts or sports. The richness of our culture is, in the words of Robert Nesta Marley, O.M., a "Pimper's Paradise," mined by those who disdain us.

One of the saddest realizations is that Africans in this country are more armed than we have ever been in our history and we are more frustrated and blood-thirsty than our forbears could have imagined. We have almost completely forgotten our history. So, as Angela Shannon writes in "To Brother Malcolm," "the Middle Passage becomes the first page"—a first page that we continually find ourselves re-living. Our outlooks are so determined by white destructiveness that we have become more and more confused, more and more like those who despise us. Our world is white and anti-white. We often imitate or react to those around us but rarely do we settle into our own skin—skin peels, hair treatment, nose-, lip- and butt-jobs the least of it. Do we know the structures at Zimbabwe, the civilizations in Dahomey and Benin, Egypt and Ethiopia, Haiti and Bahia? Do we know the Bible? Do we know who we are?

To Do

Make sure it is a little sunnier
tomorrow afternoon—do not forget
to carry an umbrella just in case;
remember, pay electric bill, and let

the landlords know the ceiling hole
has widened some; if Granny still has not
received that letter, phone her not to fret,
I will re-mail it before I leave this room;

set up that interview; avail myself
to all my friends (there will be time, I hope,
to make a mushroom quiche); remind girlfriend
about the script; and read the horoscope.

■ *April 8, 1991 : Chicago, Illinois*

What to do with old white women

What to do with old white women,
the ones who recoil from you on the bus
or in airports, the ones for whom your
business suit and attaché case

are much too much. You can sneer
at them, or spit in their faces, the way
they abased your grandparents—but
brittle bones can't take that lashing.

You can stare deep into their lizard eyes
and say "Jump!" as they clutch
their pocketbooks with varicose veins
and cooked-lobster melanoma,

but then others may think that
you're too serious. Walking upright,
without tremble, you can decline to help
them cross intersections, hoping to view

raccoon guts ironed, lab-like, into
the pavement. But no, that's too graphic—
just wish them a nice day, and smile.

■ *September 1, 1991 : Chicago, Illinois*

Mama

For Lucy, that's what
they call her

They have been gone so long now, your
children, that they do not recognize you.
Are these your children that laugh
at your cataracts? Are these your children
the ones who strike at you and bid you run
after them? The ones to whom your fingers
gave charge to stand, to sit on their stools?
Are these the babes to whom you read
the psalms and proverbs? They do not know
you now—scrawny hands, cotton hair and all.

After missiles, missives, fired your way
their glee gives way (slightly) to faint
resemblances. A pause. Then, poor orphans
finding biological parents, orphans grown
among the wildebeest and other hosts,
they come home with even more vengeful hands,
plucking at your bosom, stealing your food
and cursing you (the early manners worn off).
Your hands clasp tight in genuflection,
they already know about the Phoenix,
what lessons can you teach them, now?

■ *June 14, 1991 : Chicago, Illinois*

5

Letter to my brother

When they cross the street before they pass you,
do not be offended. It is not you that they are afraid of—
16-years-old, with a high-top fade and kenté scarf—
they are afraid of their own graphs and coördinates.
It is not you who deliberately gave smallpox-
infected blankets to frigid and trusting 'Indians,'
it is not you who fed a hundred million bodies
to the sharks which define the mercantile trade winds.
No, you did not perform 'biological tests' at Auschwitz
or in the ghettoes of Warsaw or Washington.

Lee, you must remain firm, unbowed—you must
walk with neither a hiccup nor a spasm in your step.
For when they hold up a mirror to your face—
place it on presidential campaign ads or in police albums—
it is only Frankenstein seeking his true genius.
And when they flag you down on I-95 or the Pike,
and ram a night-stick into your rib-cage, hands
behind your back and Gestapo boots grinding your neck,
you will know the bottomlessness of their power,
and they think that your hatred runs just as deep.
You must walk well, Lee, head high even if maimed.

In the elevator, those women are really not afraid of you—
their first definition of carnal twitching, unctuous savagery—
because they know what their fathers have done to Sister,
not even four hundred or a hundred years ago, but yesterday.
They know that their daddies were on the lacrosse team
when all seven peeled ears of corn and sprayed cum in her face,
then dragging her by the hair, face-down, from room to room.
So when these ladies cringe and gasp and are about to faint,
bury your smile, swallow, and know that you are not a hyena
or shaggy ogre prowling across their Savannah, just
a teenager whose very skin wears their daddies' little secrets.

Through grating holes

On January 18, at eight-twenty-six,
Rasheeda Moore, FBI lure
implored the Mayor to have a fix.

The shadow star blurred this b-grade porn—
suspenders tight, elbows at right angles,
as if to dazzle on a Coltrane horn,

but his embouchure pressed another pipe.
What now, what then, will you say to the children?
You, a spindly victim of set-up vipers?

What now, what then, can you say to your son
of ten? That Daddy was doomed in a hotel room?
That Daddy would call such a prostitute, 'Hon'?

After seven years and forty million
spent, the Feds had had you sucking mad,
chomping like a toothless old man on pudding

(but you are not as neat as that).
Your claim: when cameras roll through grating holes
all one needs is blackface, tophat?

■ *March 4, 1991 : Chicago, Illinois*

Birth

I

after Lincoln K. A. Schatz's
Fertility, 1989

s that the window or the TV? There is no sound.
Just graphic silence and five-second vignettes,
grainy and grating.
Flickering sirens, angels of blue and white fluorescence,
encircling chopper blades, infrared condors.
A yellow bandage reads: POLICE LINE. DO NOT CROSS.

There is no sound. Just the purplish blueblack of a movie studio,
brooding. "Darling, I think you breathe like the Riviera. Shall we
find out?" Rat-a-tat-tat. Graphic stutter, spasmodic heartbeats
and a teeny bird cupped in the hands, a fluttering prayer:
Synaesthesia, anaesthesia, take me out to Polynesia.

Lights swim in heroic slow motion, like X-mas semaphores.
Rat-a-tat-tat. The darkness shattered by ejaculata, the light
lingering, dancing on the insides of eyelids, disappearing
the illusion it's not—lingering afterthought. Is that the window
or the TV? Flick. Fleck. Flock. It's no Grandpa with a Winchester
and they are game but not birds.

Parents say they will give all for their children, lovers all
for each other, but what now? "Darling you hold your hem
like a schoolgirl, head sideways and swaying like a swing,
or some Third World woman washing clothes by the river.
Shall we go and find out?" Synaesthesia, anaesthesia,
     take me out...

The picture books scroll up: Anansi the Spider and Bredda Rabbit,
rippling King Arthur and the Faerye Queen. Rat-a-tat-tat.
The thunder shook so hard last week our house trembled,
the china cabinet a choral cacophony. "Darling,
Saharan lions may wish to be solitary but I don't want to be alone.
Shall we find out?" Synaesthesia, anaesthesia, take me...

Memory scrolls up further: genies and duppies, Ali Baba
and the aquiline, elfish nose of Socrates.
A ball bumps along the ground and anxious laces
rise in expansive breath behind, hurtling together
like bodies in a relay race. The Earth opens up—
a giant mouth just as in the cartoon shows,
and swallows the ball, slurps some hustling traces.

I laughed; and pissed on myself. Rat-a-tat-tat. "Darling, your eyes
...the stained glass of harlequin windows. Can we...?" Rat-a-tat-tat.
I wait for the earth to spit out my schoolmates. That cartoon is unfair.
Synaesthesia, anaesthesia...Rat-a-tat-tat. I wait. "Darling..."

■ *December 31, 1989 : Chicago, Illinois*

Toys and Candy

They have come, come. Come to free us.
The door is broken, broken down

A Grenada beat

and a pool of blood settles beside.
My father lies, lies, bleeding through the nose
and mouth, dripping like a caulked spring.
Seven bullets have carved their prints into his head.
My mother and sister were dragged away,
they said the ladies must help pay for freedom.

My lips are still bruised; their fists told me
that whatever dad taught me is iniquitous,
Dad, they said, will be buried in the village
with the other evil men.
For my forthcoming tenth birthday
they gave me toys and candy,
and said,
"Merry Christmas! You're free!"

■ *October 23, 1983 : Brooklyn, New York*

But the Pope

Βut the Pope—he said
you had no soul, Mum,
that you couldn't. No
animals can. And the "Indians,"

they're humans but could
never own them anyway. So,
why must I now fear the spirit-
snatcher, soul-snapper man?

Can a camera really freeze-
frame me—suck my soul
out? Its double click and
reeling in reminds me of

Saturday nights behind
Sticky's when Charmaine
is about to read her man.

In 1992, in the hills outside
Mexico City where few remember
the names of conquistadores,

there are four types of guilty
suspects: la bruja (sorcerer), una
comunista, un traficante

de drogas y un Protestante.
The dogs that sniff him out
are the terminating jury.

So, Mum, they kept
you as a pet around
the house, their mulatto
pickaninny, because

Irish Whiskers had tied
your mother to a pole
and danced around it?
Did you come by a soul

then? Did convict blood
make you human then?
Did it give you freckles
of blood-mold melanoma?

■ *September 20, 1991 : Chicago, Illinois*

Board Meeting, Chairman Flax

"Today we must confront a recurrent thorn
well-documented by our Research Department,
one that is hard for grand wizards to transform
so we urge you now: do not miss this appointment!

The night I was born (I swear)
the moon turned a fire-red
Jimi Hendrix,
"Voodoo Chile"

"Now, in some proper circles, academic squares,
the subject be crass if not raised with subtlety.
But when you're so right there's no need to be polite
about such crimes—the issues are too grave for tea!

"We've bowed low and mobbed them, yet the negro
problem persists without pause—in fact it's on the rise!
Our forty years at Tuskegee—the hemisphere
has seen five hundred—yet they multiply like flies!

"We feed them (baboons!), we send our goon squads
to occupy their daughters' bodies, hearts and souls
we pay and pray for them, we bleach them white
yet they remain in darkness—it's out of control!

"We cage them left, we cage them right, but all it does
is make them happy. Yes, they seek their leaders from
those places like Rikers Island and Alcatraz
just name the jailbirds—Garvey, King, and Malcolm X.

"They poison our good youth (like Socrates did) with
false ideas and other maladies—the kids must know
our greatest people—not the latest hip-hop waltz.
Now—let's finalize a solution. It's apropos."

■ *May 26, 1990 : Chicago, Illinois*

This One

T his one I dedicate to Chairman Flax
Grand Wizard, Grand Dragon of white fire
this one is for you, Buckra,[1]
for your melanin fears and thin skin
for your film transparency, flimsy negatives—
I can see clear through you.

You wish that I would have desires
to twist and bend inside your sister
till she spoke in some primal twang,
or to approach your mother in some garage—
a tall, tall shadow gliding, sliding along—
but that's not my program, Scruffy.

You wish that I would circumcise you
and ram ram ram—till you bleed some more—
but I have too many things to do.
I know—I know. It's a density thing.
You command me to make me understand
what Leanita meant when she wanted

to blow up every wan face on the bus
(put some ruddiness into these northern winds);
you dare me to pump an Uzi and perforate
my insignia through your pallid chest,
initial a jacket that's never to be worn—
keep drooling those nightmares on your pillow, Buddy.

Oh, yea, you want me to bark at you
when you say bow-wow; to grunt with you
when you scratch your balls; to fart with you
when you open your mouth—that I do do.
You got into Leanita's head and made her
take herself out—that's the hard way, you know.

I work my own schedule, HannibalOverTime
and do things with effective minimal effort.
The knowledge that you think I lack
I already know. The next time I meet
you on some cross-burning lawn, you
will have a lot to learn, once and for all.

■ *June 12, 1990 : Chicago, Illinois*

Song of Salomon Brothers

I

For Sofia, at lunch

he scene: a "war room" where a chairman
(Who has just added CEO)
Is courting winks by where he thinks
His hallowed inc. should go:

"Break down that spine-like Wall of China,
Shake tittle-tattle-tweedle-dum,
(Should you not raze it like our phrase
We'll coat Beijing with bubble-gum!)
Enlist a crop for soda pop
(Which soon will opt to exercise
The human call to consume all).
Let's watch them watch our futures rise.
Just think of it, one billion fit
To titillate such sheer elation,
Including losses after taxes—
Profits by my calculation.

"Tear down that beastly Wall of East,
Pare down that shackled-snake contraption
Which winds its way about Wuwei,
(And haul the ruins home for auction).
Gentlemen, urge the president
To settle on the less-strident side,
A scathing tongue will grate all wrongly,
So let up on those diatribes.
Go, tell him early instead to hurl
Some compliments at deadman Mao,
Let him laugh a fitful cough
To note the hiccups of the Tao.

"What hysterics to wrap generics
And sell without a tiff or pother!
Let go all cares except for shares
And the business of our fathers'.
Unseat that Wall for a western Street
With corporate gratuities,
(Don't let it out, we plan without
Assessing the annuities).

"The stint ahead is when to spread
And how to best diversify;
(Regardless who may question you
Go bid the Chinese multiply!)
Let's set this market as our target
To sell our noble pioneering,
Create some need for paddy seeds
Of genetic engineering.
(New York may rattle as we straddle
Along Milken Avenue,
While we're winning, a dead fish grinning
Will logo all that we've been through.)
Set sail for Thailand or Huang Hai
To patronize a puppet show,
(Being not natives of Brunei
We could be sultans of—Soho?)

"Since interest rates appreciate
On mere intangibles, meagre hopes,
I'll gladly bet on téte-â-tétes
With worldly leaders, even popes,
When China tears the lining hair
Which binds her belly to the ground
Like neutron tufts against her back—
Rise up and comb your cumber down!
Make no mistake, do not forsake
Our gravity of intention.
No liberal ass from my language class
Would cancel out an intervention.

"I could continue to highlight revenue
As our *primum mobile* thing
To lift some cash. —We've got to dash!
The Market bell's about to ring!
[More good news, partners, for my worth,
My wife is pregnant—so I've heard!
Soon to leave her one more consumer
In Pritcher Apricot, the 3d.]"

■ *September 11, 1987 : New Haven, Connecticut*

Fragments for Walcott

With screaming engines an aeroplane slices through
the thick heat which stagnates like a genie's garment,
sliding its shadow over rectangular cane-fields,
combing the country's green hair
which sway outside the window like obedient
seaweed answering waves:

> the scene, a child's plaything.

The silver jet, needling in and out of clouds,
threading azure circles with its cotton contrails,
glares its underbelly in the New York twilight.
And Derek, a granted scholar known to punctuate
cocktail conversations with his "exotic" tongue,
glances out of his pane towards the Empire State Building:
"Maybe the critics will like my creation, maybe
they'll visit the hills and gullies, the tintinnabulation
of the sun on steel pans and zinc roofs, but not as tourists.
After all, one may produce more in two months of blatant
colonization than a craftsman would in, say, Rome,
where patrons are apt to instruct me. But their
natural sways are all on reserve, overnight, three-day,
lifetime reserve. Our plants in buckets, our
parks fenced off in the city where stained
cranes are inured to green water."

Two steps down from the plane and a stone's throw
from Kennedy, another derrick, roaring
like a menstrual dinosaur, punches pockets into buildings.
His metamorphosis is instinctive, a nudge. He knows—
he knows the halo of haze wraps him:
      the crane can't raze the dust.
And maybe the camera flashes will not be so flitting,
not all magazine pages turn yellow.

The needle sprain of the ankle pricks him,
a crayfish pegging the flesh like an orange.
The thoughts do not flow in the empire,
though they bristle like dammed-up, damned floods.
And suppose the bowery is not bankrupt,
suppose the ideas are not as frustrated as the city streams?

The spires of the World Trade Center
      still prick the Cosmos—
puncturing the haze which bandages New York.
Pillared banks and cathedrals attract an equal number
      of pilgrims.

Wall Street friends pray for simulations of Armageddon
(sell everything short for gold will go up!).
Automaton laborers scuttle to work, ever
so importantly, where they are calmly awaited
by detached, periscopic camera eyes,
and the ever so important smell of coffee.

■ *April 28, 1985 : Brooklyn, New York*

Dreams in Soy Sauce

1.

Mum, my dearest grand mamaa, slumps
over a pail bleaching clothes, the bubbles
pop beneath her fingers (squish-squish,
squish-squish like a croaking lizard).
Her back is turned towards me and as I
approach her left side she says, "The floor,
the floor. I've cleaned and waxed the floor—
it shines beautifully!" Mum's neck ripples
like a turkey's. She ordinarily does not
say anything with such force. I have not seen
or written to her for a year or so. Her head still
bowed, she squints softly, "I'm pissed at you."

2.

At the nightclub, they stab people who dance
on the staggered steps of the stage, stab them
in the legs. A Eurasian singer, smothered
with ashen foundation, flings his hair and beats
his head against a patient steel pole in a cage—
his teeth bared and bloody. I have only come to dance.

A dire deconstructionist from New Haven,
(black lipstick, cigarette black) plants a ratchet
into my left calf, leaving a too-anxious gush
in its wake. I kick him in the face, grab the knife,
and take off.

3.

Then find myself on a train through
Greenwich, behind a day school with a cricket pitch,
blazoned copper. The carillon chimes us to dinner.
A young bowler in starched white reddens
his trousers while shining the ball on his pocket.
I ask him, googly or leg-breaker? Spin ball or pace?
He does not answer; but a pasted spectator,
the one from that same nightclub, offers something
to drink. I run away from her to find myself
in a West Side disco on the Hudson where
it is always night. Some guards, fingers dangling,
question my pass and ask each other if I had a right
to keep the knife. (I did not realize it was in my hand.)
They examine my gash, skin up their faces half-
smelling something, half-pleasured, and nod.
I may come in.

4.

In Provincetown, another cut-out paste-up (white face,
all-black eyes) streams up and spills out of a Spider,
a play-car really. She is squired by a linebacker
who dashes into a carpet store. They must want
their knife back. I panic. I have lost it. The lineman
comes out of the shop and hails a cop-car
as if it were a cab. They wave to me with
hands that spin in board games.

■ *November 11, 1990 : Chicago, Illinois*

doctors' delight, or the dinner-makers

For Matthew Paris

The characters in white aprons,
their steely spectacles and
sharp shark eyes zooming in and out of my face,
their tongues wiping off alligator smiles,
their white gloves tuning metal utensils;
and the sirens scream (i think)
down gravesend avenue like fluttering fowls.
i feel faint flashing tints
of red and blue encircling me
like flames, or stars and angels—

my soul evaporates

(where am i?)

and floats in steam
to hover wingless above the wreath—
above the pot-rim of surgeon heads.
the soul fills out a pigeon's form and
aims for the spotless pates; soundless
air spirals down to the bulls-head,
but nothing pukey (gosh!).
the fixers then (like king vultures)
unzip my body's belly
(i rub my hands in excitement!)
and a turnip pops out
like a jack in the body.
my life bubbles boil and bellow—
the clogged blood shivers like jello;
the toller's bells begin their chime
and all the docs decide to dine.

■ *June 11, 1983 : New York, New York*

And the Tao said

Red helicopters
        hover on the horizon,
dark ideographs;

camouflaged choppers
float into the sunrise blush,
Chinese characters.

A tanned leaf dances
to earth where people
pile like bags of sand.

■ *October 24, 1983 : Brooklyn, New York*

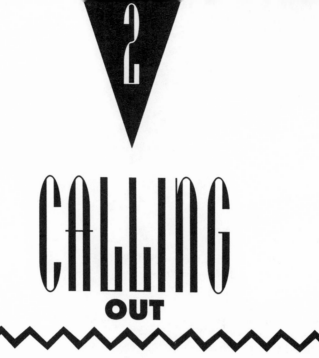

CALLING

OUT

In some studies of black men who were electrocuted during the 1930s and 40s, the recorders noted that these men would yell out the name of Joe Louis just before their death. His name, and Christ's, were the ones which tapered on their breaths. The symbolism of Joe Louis predominant on a level playing field is powerful. It is this sense of fairness and strength that stayed with these men till the very end.

Our heroes are all with us, inhabiting our house walls, our churches and other places of assembly—breathing anew for our daily strength. It is almost magical, the effect of saying their names: Sojourner, Rosa, Jesse O., Jesse J., Phyllis, Alice, Uncle Remus, Miss Lou, 'Trane and, a little late, Miles:

> Kind of blue about you, kind of miss
> the way those fingers popped big fun
> with that bitch's brew.
>
> Yea, I know your hands well,
> playing games with my spine
> throwing an arch, a net, as if
>
> it were some strange butterfly putty,
> lapping over with every whisper,
> every wink. Played all kinds
>
> of games, man, I should be mad.
> And I have gone crazy with your brush-
> notes, jazz-strokes, fused jokes—

do you really mean what they say you say?
I never really got all of it, you know,
couldn't get through the hair-cover

to see if "Amandla" was sered
into your scalp, as you said.
Miles, what's up with these folk

frowning like they got fired.
Come tell them the truth,
show them it was just a blue

mist, an illusion. You are
just kidding now. Come show them!
Blow them away again, Miles.

    Our loved ones far and wide awaken deep genius and strength in our bloodlines. Now we call to the spirits. For in this hour when the sheer paper weight of the statistics threatens to crush us, when an unending sea of people earn their doctorates on the volume of our pain, we need you more than ever. We call on Martin as we rise like a mighty stream. And on Stokely with firm hands. We call on Bob Marley for the lion rock, and on Malcolm for unflinching stance. We call on our mothers and fathers, our grandmothers and grandfathers to watch over us as we shed our laundry, our lies, our hangups and our masters.

    We know that our fate is ours and ours alone. We cannot blame those who we allow to dominate us because we have allowed it. We cannot say that we are outnumbered/outgunned/out-anything, because we can do anything we want to. Our aims must be clear, our gods omnipresent, our destiny assured.

    To the ancestors who are buried in deserts, whose bones have become oil, we drive in ignorance. To the ancestors caked onto the floors of oceans, we drink/swim/dump/urinate in ignorance. To those who have won victories which we cannot now remember, forgive us our dead brain cells—it's all been jheri-curled, relaxed, frozen out of us. We call out your names in a thousand languages and ask that you guide us. Show us where we cannot see—ultraviolet, infrared, the depths of the sea. Tell us where others are deaf. And lead us into ever-completion.

The Call

From a conversation
with A.W.S.

The night I called the police on
my father, bottles were released
against the fridge. He hadn't won
whatever, and could not be appeased
by Mommy's purr (her twitching palms
in cocoa butter) nor by my pleas.

When chilled, my mother was well-
behaved about those thumps to mid-
section. Silence did not tell
the doctor why she miscarried,
silence did not help the counselor
help the child already hidden.

The night I called the police to
arrest my father, there was no
consideration about who
was going to say what, and how
the neighbors who had a view
would tell the tale to so-and-so,

because my little sister's hands
were hammering their prints across
a corner wall, because the man
(as Daddy would skin up his face)
the bleeping walkie-talkie man
could singe a name on Father's rass.

The night I asked the cops to cuff
his hands / my hands behind his back / my back
I only heard wheezing and coughing
and china crackling, crink-crank-crack
and Mommy barking: rough, so rough!
I only heard the biffs and thwacks
and I, too, had had enough.

■ *November 23, 1990 : Chicago, Illinois*

Response

When officers arrive to cart
off your parent, do not expect
them to know the times that father
turned on all the bathroom faucets
and wept; these cops cannot count
the three packs of cigarettes

sucked in each day in your name
as if those artificial rings—
the threads of yarn, that eland crown—
could divine a ladder up from
the stoop. When officers begin
the questioning, they have forgotten

that their parents and grand parents
also have warm skin, they have for-
gotten that deep-set eyes, deep-set
darkness can absorb—absorb their words,
and yes, he has sinned, but he's not
an ox or donkey, he's not a mangy cur

although his voice grows puppily soft.
Invited strangers to your home
may note a tidy couch, more often
they will record the dirt strewn
between a crack that has just begun
to splinter when the squad-cars come.

■ *November 23, 1990 : Chicago, Illinois*

Lovesong to Jimi Hendrix

I know that you are humming, brother,
like radial tires over the iron grid of a bridge
high-gear, high-speed take-off

for Seth MacLowry

I show that you are coming, rather
silent as a thought, without a grudge
for those that laughed at your runny nose

but don't wait too long, Jimi, for I'm strumming
my belly button window and biting strings.
Come soon, before I become a too-bumming mother—

■ *November 1, 1990 : Chicago, Illinois*

Plath Poem

Let this paling palm not be an-
other lapel pin for your soirées
and expositions (sandpaper voice,
acute snips), another show of urtication—
by osmosis if not by your own skin.
I may hold it as you held me: in ice water.

Let my bloomed pupils not fix on
hands dragging over drawn faces, slowly
so that the veins wake like worms.
Let visitors not say that they knew me
when they march off with my memories
"O, X was so dear, dear—Oh, was X—?"
I would see it as they strained me:
through sneezes and onion eyes.

Replace the grains in the hourglass
with this crematory dust—
let the trickle be a whisper
to live by, speckling your silences
with my cauterized carbon.

■ *November 1, 1990 : Chicago, Illinois*

Letter from Foreign

Dear Mum, there are so many things I have
to tell 'bout 'Merica, the place where you said
the streets are gold and there are many people
with good hair (like those in the movies).

for A. W. S.

'Member when I use to play with the toy helicopter
and fly away a foreign? Well, Mum, Dearest Grand Mamaa,
I have some news for you. 'Merica is not in the sky
like the planes but is on land, flat land, droopy corn-fields
and choking chimneys, with latrines, and doo-doo
and frowsy ragamuffins as good as dead on sidewalks.

Mum, you tell me say God bless America for the people
here good, I have some more news for you.
Sure, some people go to church and chapel
and mosque and synagogue and march and pray
and some smile when they see you on the street
(some don't say 'Morning, dog' and sometimes
them cross the street when we pass them—
for an healthy Black man is a dinosaur
blowing fire at the people with pretty hair
and you know how easy it is for hair to catch fire.)

Mum, you tell me that they have scholarships galore.
And, a true. But you never say anything 'bout glass,
'bout aquarium and how buckra can encase you
in glass so that no matter how loud you scream
no matter how much you bark, the ceiling still there.

I don't want to bring down God on me so I must say
that education here good and that we learn all kinds
of things 'bout Greece and Rome, me speak Italian
now, some French—even Japanese. All these things
that you wanted me to do, Mum, but there is lots of glass about,
lenses, ceilings, bottles and they're all trained on me, you know,
reflecting, watching, waiting and laughing,
but I have to follow your lead, almost a century
and still not weary yet, I must never get weary yet.

■ *October 15, 1989 : Chicago, Illinois*

In the Pores of Soweto

His member dangles like a worm between
a belly-buster's beak, hurried like an

For Carlton Henry Reid

umbilical cord plucked by vultures—
O, yes! O, yes, the hungry ones have come
in the pores of Soweto.

In the pores of Soweto—in the pores of their home.
In the pores of Soweto...Soweto their home.

My grandma is great. I love her so
I always agree with her: Yes, Nana,
that was Marcus and Cleo at lunch today,
they were listening—Shaka listened also.

Yes, Nana, Papa will be returning
soon, they took him to get some awards—
that motorcade was just to keep admiring
crowds away, not to leave him, not

to leave him on Robben Island for thirty years.
I sometimes must clarify to my old lady
things picked up from the truant children
(how mustard gas raises the skin—lifts it up—

and what it does to eyes—to eyes)—things which
she wants no memory of. Invariably,
the conversation continues: Yes, Nana. Nelson
will come for tea this afternoon. Yes, Nana,

you do hear the bells but that means Makela
has gone to the church today, that Gatsha
will marry into that family you love, that
Linda was not shot at school this morning.

Only seven, her grandchild has taken to acting
like Nana too, has taken to a cane which
has not taken to her. As she plays police
it becomes that knife, that gun, that altar, God.

Girls and boys sing work songs, heaving
and breaking rock stones, daily digging
graves and preparing tombs for the little ones—
scattered wild seeds in the pores of Soweto.

■ *April 7, 1991 : Chicago, Illinois*

dam

f now as I ripple to your bank
that wind should sip
and over this cliff
spit me onto that rock—
catcher of all that falls—
splashing, splintering me
onto barks and leaves,
would you care?
would i just water trees?

■ *April 23, 1979 : St. Mary, Jamaica*

Macoute

A Haitian simmer

Monkey Man of immaculate teeth, cheeks
so red and fiery they fuse with your
eyes. Monkey Man Baba wiping your
cutlass on a grindstone, ping-ping,
I wait for the last dinosaur
to turn to
stone,
to turn to
lime, you Monkey Mime.

■ *July 2, 1990 : Chicago, Illinois*

36

An Ant

with due apologies

A pallid pad was sitting square against the shadow of my pen; a former here, another there, but only lovers roamed my ken. I scratched my head for giddy dreams to see how lithely X had danced. My hispid neck was quite serene, until the creepings of an ant. It ran about the hair or two which loosened with my fingertips; its limbs were of a brownish blue—this pismire jutted clawish lips. I eyed it half-way up the page and saw it magnified in films: what monster from that flying age (I plotted now to detach its limbs).

I turned the bugger on its back and watched it pray, or cry, or beg. I questioned toes and suction tracks, and wondered more then tore a leg. The troubled rascal did a wheel as if to mime an axle rod. Such wounds, I thought, would quickly heal, especially for an arthropod. I tore another from the side and thus its spin reversed in trend. At first it twirled the bottom hide, but now it swirls the other end. A dancer or a top could not have spun for long in that bed; it spindled in a lover's knot. A little bored, I spiked the head.

■ *March 29, 1987 : New Haven, Connecticut*

Fat people should not take the bus

And I don't
mean to sound
like a svelte
snob with that.
Nor is it mean
for you to laugh
at the creaks
when fatty
boom-booms
fling their blobs
to occupy a
whole seat
and a half.

■ *July 2, 1990 : Chicago, Illinois*

38

McLove

anted: a male (S and M)
who shuts his eyes when kissing
or kneeling at a prayer pew
(not religious, per se, but *very* inspired).

If you are rich (B and W)
and into Chinese kittens
Arctic haunts, Cayman isles,
non-smoker with no hair—

then send your photo
to the matchbox below.
Druggies, derelicts—don't even try
(writers also need not apply).

■ *May 27, 1991 : Chicago, Illinois*

Lie

for Carmine Giordano

Some televangelists, with kleigs and all,
Propose to lecture on my porch,
And you with churchly wherewithal
Have joined to shine the holy torch;

Should I, with stockings flung behind
My head, and panty-tangled feet,
Revere the hymns you sing, or bind
Myself in bliss beneath these sheets?

And when you say the world is wrecked
By sinners, duds, and rosy rods,
Should I, my dear, unseam my neck
To sacrifice my blood for gods?

And when you cast a curse on me
To tell me that my days are done
(Because, you say, I cannot see
Where sky and land and god are one),

I look above and then below
And to the house where pilgrims go,
Then kneel to clasp your breast in prayer
And sanctify my pleasures there.

The flailing, grief, the nails and strife—
I postpone for some other life.

■ *November 2, 1984 : Brooklyn, New York*

40

Devotion

Ihe other day while consciously
consecrating a creaking bed,

to Cynthia

a pristine priest came up to me
to iterate what he had said.
He held the scriptures in his hands
and thundered loud on Heaven's Way.
I broke, he said, a few commands
because I had not gone to pray.
I gazed at him beneath the sweat
that raced in torrents down my face
and asked myself, did he forget?
Or does he long to have my place?
For all the pilgrims that I know
are sure to come before they go.

Besides, I thought, what else should I,
mere mortal who obeys the psalms,
revere more, so as to touch the sky,
than someone's breast between my arms.
"It is divine," the father spoke,
"for man to love his fellow mate,
but you, young sinner, have revoked
the word of Jesus and your faith,
and since you're only seventeen—
although you grunt like twenty-one—
I know the little you've seen
so heed the gospels of St. John."
His readings poked about my soul
and also made my lover whole.

■ *November 20, 1984 : New York, New York*

Big Daddy on Raft

y nodding head will calmly plead
That you are charged for me:
All rivers sing and always bring
Their currents to the sea.
All streams, my love, have leagues to move
Before they near the mouth,
But ocean dear, is waiting here,
In deluge or in doubt.
And since your course of deep remorse
Reflects a deepened blue,
You must decide to splash aside
The riffraff who you rue,
Or else, my dear, your waterbed steam
Will flit away like sun-lit dreams.

■ *July 30, 1985 : Brooklyn, New York*

3

MARROW
TO MOUTH

The box is a frank thing. Dictionaries note its confining and enclosing qualities, its static monoplanes and teeth-gritting texture. Its very shape bespeaks a utilitarian squareness and linear functionality. Its pressure points meet, like fault lines of a volcano, to erupt outward—directing arrows up and down from frictional geometric coördinates.

In his mid-1980s manuscript working-titled, *Missile and Capsule*,[1] the poet/historian/scholar (Edward) Kamau Brathwaite argues that the box is the quintessential European idea.[2] It dominates the construction of houses, schools, acres, military strategies, ways of thought. It implies a start, a progress, and a definitive end. The box teased out, through the steeples and spires that mark religious, commercial and other structures, exhibit an ever-outward sensing, the invisible sensing of the prostrate blind. The undergirding world view—whether it is to find God or new markets—is that values are alien to the being and must be captured from without.[3]

The circle, on the other hand, is the representative African paradigm.[4] It is interior and self-reflective. All its forces beam inward. Whereas the box functions best in technological and material development which require linear logic and assembly-line timetables, the circle's values are realized in relation to culture and the spirits. The circle not only mimics the outer cosmos, but our spirit selves as well.[5] Many African cultures share the belief that humans possess divinity within ourselves and it is up to us, through living in harmony with all material and immaterial things and calling out our essences, to attain our full selves.

The circle of the drum/bass and the dance it presupposes shows us the way. (Can you imagine a square drum?) Its concentricity is another manifestation of our inner structure, the layers and layers which must be broken down so that we can get to the spirit, to reach the absolute core where we are at one with our consciousness, our environment and our cosmos. The bass/drum is then symbolic of our cultures, because it is through its languages that we speak to each other across the Diaspora, across the accents and clicks, across the deserts and seas. Whether it is to announce the pan season in

Trinidad, Carnaval in Brazil, a marriage in Senegal, a harvest in Ghana, or war against evil in South Africa, we can understand its languages. Whether it is through hip-hop sub-woofers in Brooklyn and the Bronx, reggae sound systems in Kingston, Mo'Bay or Tokyo, or symphony orchestras in Philadelphia or Washington, we can feel it around our navels and in our stomachs. We can sense the calls of a mystic return and rebirth. We know where we want to go and it draws us with a fateful/faithful frequency.

Music is our first literature and culture. Babies sing their "nonsense syllables" and we try to communicate with them by singing back. The "insane" make wild music. Those in possession wail out from deep wellsprings. When we cry, we cry in song. When we rejoice, we rejoice in song. The drum as music banishes our ills and spiteful thoughts, our hang-ups and downpression. It speaks to our endemic divinity, riddling our souls with spirit-releasing sounds, so that we may properly be strengthened and purified and at peace with our polychromatic, synaesthetic selves. We can then do whatever needs to be done. We can see, feel, smell and taste the drum, and it informs us on levels that we cannot name. But we know that music makes us closer to being whole. Much of our quest throughout oral, written and painted history has been to loosen the rings around our souls. And the drum is the ultimate shaker, the penultimate rattler of those bells.

Music

B
urning Spear wails with a hole, a hollow, in his voice
a strained strain, taut from squeezing out the sound,
de sound
de soun':[1] *Marcus Garvey words come to pass.*[2]
Tired of the echoes, Mau-Mau[3] bawling from Mount Kenya,
tired of the waiting and politicians, shegries[4] and lies:
See the hypocrites them a galong deh.[5]

But a no so i fi go
that is not the way things should be

Burning Spear has a chasm in his voice—
not an abyss, mind you—but a big gap nonetheless
through which Nanny and Sam Sharpe, Harriet, Frederick
Toussaint and Eric Williams—the long line of Maroons[6]
stream up; where Paul Bogle tells the colonial tribunal
(him never did have any sort of fair hearing, you know)
tell today's jury, how them hang him for asking:
*Am I not...*But him couldn't go no further
"Black" and "Man" no fit too well in the same sentence
(*You favor flying pattoo,*[7] *you favor...*)
For that was the sentence, the missionary terms
for a Cain, canine

Sister Nanny up there in Cockpit Country inventing guerilla war-
fare and bleeding herself free of the plantation
Them say she work obeah, pocomania and vodoun[8]
them say a black magic, heathen whispers make her strong
make her catch bullets with her behind and fart them out.
But it beat back the British, no? If a poco make her 'trong
come work 'pon me, High Priestess come sing
make the woofers loosen the knots/gnats/knots in my stomach
warm the showers every time Babylon glowers at me

You see these little Caribbean islands sailing away,
sculpted like beautiful tourist postcards,
these little irregular punctuations in the sea
connected by vast amounts of salt and water
nutritious from the bones of the Middle Passage

Do you remember the days of slavery [9]

these little lands created by blowing bubbles
no make them fool you—them too small
to contain the voices, too small to hold the history
think of the water instead

Burning Spear has a hollow in his voice
the spirits much too big for the media, cracking
spilling the ancestors onto digital
harvest moon and juk-kunnu[10]
exploding guts, tar, feather, cat-o-nine tails

But a no so i' fi go

When the rain stops falling down
And they ain't go no water
They're gonna bow down to the ground
Wishing that they were under

When the stars start falling off
And the fire is burning (red hot)
There will be a weeping and gnashing of teeth
At four in the morning [11]

Hear the names of the dancehall dee-jays
Shabba Ranks and Lieutenant Stitchie sewing up the wounds
Ninja Man and Daddy Lizard at Cross Roads
Shelley Thunder with the (small) double axe of Shango

See the South African school children
girls in blue dresses, boys in khaki uniforms
pounding the toyi-toyi[12] in the streets of Soweto
their feet trotting on grapes and vineyards
plotting a bitter wine

Nelson free, Nelson free, we feel irie
Them free Mandela out a penitentiary

Deep, deep down in the diamond dunes
drilling, digging and drowning in dust
close to the stimela fields
all across the hinterland
ploughing the crenelated veldt
and feeling the master's sjambok
wipe across back and belly,
back!back!back!
welting, wailing, draping them up
John Crow[13] and rolling-calf duppy[14]
blap!blap!blap!

But a no so i' fi go

P.E. penultimate—all the voices coming out
squirming like worms, squeezed through telephone
and PA system: *Public Enemy Number One*
through the steel pipes of Rikers and Compton,
Spofford and Alcatraz—bloody ass, Babylon
the pimp, the warden smiles widely
there's weed growing among his teeth
may look like it, but the ancestor has not returned.

■ *October 22, 1989 : Chicago, Illinois*

Them Days

I ake me back to Ol' Virginny
where the boys are strong
and the women so skinny—

just give me some of them grand ol' days:

when everything happened in black and white
when tin-pan voices were flat and cheery,
submerged in cushions of static,
and everyone's walk was a twitch or a throb.

The diamond days of Garbo and Gable
lazy breezes fluffing out the cotton curtains
when Shirley Temple danced with Mr. Bojangles
her equal, and there was no VHF or cable.

Anyone of note was named Sam then—
his walk would become the inseam, in-swing;
little boys wore plaid on their paper routes
while the fog was sliced by saxophones all over town.

We had no color or 3-D then.
All the Negroes were happy so, skipping
into the fields, happy as kangaroos
my, look how well they dance, even to the blues—

the Orientals were squinting like lizards
with their old kung fu thing

and we were all living the American dream.

Take me back to Nineteen-Twenty
when the coloreds were wrong
and we pegged them aplenty.

Triangle Trade, Triangle Legs

1.

■ From the frigate, the plashing's primary
brown bodies bob and glisten under moon-glow
bulged eyes moon-dance, flick-fleck, like shards
of mirror shaking off splinter-blades of light,

splashing arms, muted cries like cracking saxophones
filling up with air bubbles—plop, plop, plop
fizzling soda water shall never taste the same.

The possession of the undertow—circular, sensuous
masks repeated jabs and forays of teeth, jigga-jigga
great white sharks stripping blueblack bodies to bones
jawing, jarring, sawing from underneath.

What happened to the skulls thrown overboard?
Did they organize themselves like the shelves
of the Khmer Rouge, layer after layer of calcifying crania?

Did they settle like bearing balls into
assembly-line tracks along the ocean floor
prepared to bear another galley of cargo?

Where do they rest? Where do they rest
after fish have fleeced the flesh?
Fossilizing, petrifying into future oil
deposits to propel missiles and spaceships?

Salt water, O sacred burial ground

The oilman laps up the sea with an electric tongue
raking over the cemetery, even now
cracking, belittling the bones, still not at peace.

2.

In the reggae and mento songs at the hotel
they pour out homilies to the trade winds
mystical and sweet, these sunburnt

shiny old men smelling of camphor oil
mint tea and rum, tongues across unsteady teeth
like solo fingers along piano keys
pain, me say pain-o
pain a come and me wan go home
digits on rusty banjo, scraping donkey jawbones
as haloed, hallowed tourists skank and rub-a-dub

dance nah done till a morning,
pain, me say pain, woe!

■ *March 1987 : Montego Bay, Jamaica*

In A Tar-Mangled Manner

O, slave, can you flee
by the eagle's first flight
for so loudly we wail
from that whipper's fresh creaming,

A minor key

who's brought swipes and blue scars
to our tremulous thighs
and our children, we watched,
O, so helplessly screaming?

O, the lyncher's red stare—
their licks bursting in fear
burned blood through the night,
the charred fruit is still there.

O, say, is that tar-mangled
planter, that slave,
still in the hands of debris
that have come from the caves?

■ *March 22, 1991 : Chicago, Illinois*

Lift Every Fist And Swing

Lift every fist and swing
till all their mouths cave in
cave in like crockery
breaking in liberty.

Let our pounding rise
swell up their devilish eyes,
let it resound with the glee
of waves in the sea.

Swing a blow, full of the horrors
that their hate has brought us;
swing one low, tear at the terror
that these rapists have taught us.

Facing their laser guns
dark shadows on the run
let us run on until
we fell a final kill...

■ *March 22, 1991 : Chicago, Illinois*